Communicating

Speaking and Listening to End Misunderstanding and Promote Friendship

Dale R. Olen, Ph.D.

D1508876

A Life Skills Series Book

JODA Communications, Ltd.
Milwaukee, Wisconsin

Editor: Carolyn Kott Washburne
Design: Chris Roerden and Associates
Layout: Eileen Olen

ISBN 1-56583-007-5

Published by: JODA Communications, Ltd.
10125 West North Avenue
Milwaukee, WI 53226

PRINTED IN THE UNITED STATES OF AMERICA

Table of Contents

Introduction

to the
Life Skills Series

Nobody gets out alive! It isn't easy navigating your way through life. Your relationships, parents, marriage, children, job, school, church, all make big demands on you. Sometimes you feel rather ill-equipped to make this journey. You feel as if you have been tossed out in the cold without even a warm jacket. Life's journey demands considerable skill. Navigating the sometimes smooth, other times treacherous journey calls for a wide variety of tools and talents. When the ride feels like a sailboat pushed by a gentle breeze, slicing through the still waters, you go with the flow. You live naturally with the skills already developed.

But other times (and these other times can make you forget the smooth sailing), the sea turns. The boat shifts violently, driven by the waves' force. At those stormy moments, you look at your personal resources, and they just don't seem sufficient.

Gabriel Marcel, the French philosopher, wrote that the journey of life is like a spiral. The Greeks, he observed, viewed life as *cyclical*–sort of the same old thing over and over. The seasons came, went, and came again. History repeated itself. The Hebrews, on the other hand, saw life as *linear*–a pretty straight march toward a goal. You begin at the Alpha point and end at Omega. It's as simple as that.

Marcel combined the two views by capturing the goal-oriented optimism of the Hebrews and the sobering reality of the Greeks' cycles. Life has its ups and downs, but it always moves forward.

To minimize the *downs* and to make the most of the *ups*, you need **Life Skills**. When you hike down the Grand Canyon, you use particular muscles in your back and legs. And when you trudge up the Canyon, you use other muscles. So too with life skills. You call on certain skills when your life spirals down, such as the skill of defeating depression and managing stress. When your life is on an upswing, you employ skills like thinking reasonably and meeting life head on.

This series of books is about the skills you need for getting through life. To get from beginning to end without falling flat on your face and to achieve some dignity and some self-satisfaction, you need **basic** life skills. These include:

1. Accepting yourself.
2. Thinking reasonably.
3. Meeting life head on.

With these three life skills mastered to some degree, you can get a handle on your life. Now, if you want to build from there, you are going to need a few more skills. These include:

4. Communicating.
5. Managing stress.
6. Being intimate.
7. Resolving conflict.
8. Reducing anger.
9. Overcoming fear.
10. Defeating depression.

If you have these ten skills up and running in your life, you are ready to face yourself, your relationships, your parents, your marriage, your children, your job and even God with the hope of handling whatever comes your way. Without these skills, you are going to bump into one stone wall after another. These skills don't take away the problems, the challenges and the hard times. But they do help you dig out of life's deep trenches and more fully *enjoy* the good times.

Life Skills can be learned. You have what it takes to master each of these skills–even if you feel you don't have the tiniest bit of the skill right now. But nobody can develop the skill for you. You have to take charge and develop it yourself. Your family, friends and community may be able to help you, but you are the center at which each skill has to start. Here is all you need to begin this learning process:

- Awareness.
- The desire to grow.
- Effort and practice.

Awareness begins the process of change. You have to notice yourself, watch your behavior and honestly face your strengths and weaknesses. You have to take stock of each skill and of the obstacles in you that might inhibit its growth.

Once you recognize the value of a skill and focus on it, you have to want to pursue it. The critical principle here, one you will see throughout this series, is *desire*. Your desire will force you to focus on the growing you want to do and keep you going when learning comes hard.

Finally, your *effort and practice* will make these **Life Skills** come alive for you. You can do it. The ten books in the **Life Skills Series** are tools to guide and encourage your progress. They are my way of being with you–cheering your efforts. But without your practice, what you find in these books will wash out to sea.

Working on these ten **Life Skills** won't get you through life without any scars. But the effort you put in will help you measure your life in more than years. Your life will be measured in the zest, faith, love, honesty and generosity you bring to yourself and your relationships.

I can hardly wait for you to get started!

Chapter One

What is the Skill of Communicating?

Your world is filled with words, pictures and gestures. The voices of friends, parents, lovers, teachers, bosses, co-workers and enemies permeate your senses and flood your soul. The radio speaks and sings. The television announces. The newspapers and magazines print out words in black and white. You write a letter, send a co-worker a memo, make a phone call, tell your friend you love her. In most of your waking moments you are sending or receiving messages.

Your primary occupation as a human being is communicating. Except for breathing, there is nothing you do more frequently than get and give messages. These messages connect you with others. You have sent and received messages throughout your life because deep within you moves an energy to unite you with other parts of creation. You instinctively seek various forms of union with people and things.

The drive in you toward connecting, involving yourself in the lives of others, bonding, uniting and ultimately loving is so great, you literally spend your entire life attempting to achieve that goal. The way you reach ultimate union is through the *skill of communicating.*

In what classroom have you learned this skill? Certainly some aspects of communicating were learned in reading and writing classes, also in music and art. Perhaps in college you took a speech class. All these skills have definitely helped you give and get messages more effectively. But I'll bet that nowhere along the way did you get a course in giving and receiving messages in interpersonal relationships. How do you talk with your lover? Your parent or child? Your boss or employee? How do you make sure you're really understanding the message the other is trying to send? And how can you send messages clearly and simply enough so the other can receive them?

Now is the time to sort through your communication tools. As you read this book, you can assess your approaches to giving and receiving messages. You can decide which skills you want to keep, which you want to fine tune and which you want to throw out because they don't work. I'm delighted you have picked up this book and want to increase your skill in communicating with others. Since you communicate more than almost anything else you do, improving this skill will bring great satisfaction and enjoyment to your life. So just what is this skill of communicating?

Communication always involves *giving* and *receiving*.

Effective communication reveals a rhythm of giving and receiving. When it's happening, the flow between you and another feels balanced and in harmony. When you give, the other receives. The two of you continue changing positions until you both feel you have spoken what you wish and have been understood by the other. The principle that describes and makes communication work is stated simply: For two people to communicate, you always need a *Giver* and a *Receiver*.

While this principle appears obvious and elementary, your ability to create and maintain this rhythm is tested every day. Oftentimes the non-rhythms of communication appear instead. These non-rhythms sabotage effective verbal sharing and undercut its very purpose, which is to connect you to others. To better understand the rhythm of giving and receiving necessary for communication, let's first take a look at the four ways communication breaks down.

The Non-Rhythms of Communication

Giver–Giver: The first non-rhythm sets a *Giver* against a *Giver*. When the two of you are intent on telling each other something, neither receives well. This non-rhythm both creates and sustains conflict. Each of you experiences frustration because, as a *Giver*, you need a *Receiver*. Yet the other can't receive because he or she is also so intent on giving.

For example, when Sylvia saw the new fishing rod and tackle box sitting in the living room, her hot button went off immediately. Stan had promised her, she thought, not to spend any more money this season on fishing. She immediately went into the living room, where her husband was peacefully watching television, and let him know what she thought about his fishing purchases. In no time his hot button went off as well. He quickly went on the defensive, trying to tell Sylvia how the rod was on sale and what a bargain the tackle box was. She kept right on telling him in no uncertain terms how totally irresponsible such a purchase was, especially with all their other expenses this summer. For 15 minutes she tried to persuade him to think less selfishly about buying "toys" for himself, while he attempted to convince her of how hard he had worked for the family and that he deserved a little reward once in a while.

The discussion was deadlocked. Both Sylvia and Stan ended up yelling at each other, calling one another names. Both were ready to punch each other. Stan finally announced, "I've had it around here." He got up from his chair and stomped out of the house. That ended the non-rhythm of Giver–Giver communication.

These two people didn't hear each other at all. Both were sending messages, with neither one of them receiving. Both felt frustrated because the other wasn't getting the message. In their desire to get their messages across, they did two things:

1. They each began *repeating* themselves. In fact, most of their 15 minutes were used to repeat the one or two thoughts they had on the subject. If they had listened to each other, the discussion could have lasted about two minutes instead of 15. When you try giving a message to someone, and you think that person isn't getting it, you keep repeating it until he or she does get it.

2. They each *got louder*. Sylvia and Stan believed, incorrectly, that by speaking louder the other would hear better. The opposite was true. If someone shouts at you, your first tendency is to put your hands over your ears. It's too hard to listen. So you don't. But if the other thinks you're not listening, he or she speaks even louder, hoping to get through your deafness. If both of you are in the same mode of trying to send a message the other doesn't want to receive, the results are inevitable. Both of you end up shouting, frustrated and upset, because you can't get your point across. This dynamic results in what Eric Berne referred to as the game of "Uproar." The game ends when one of you slams a door – either physically by walking out or psychologically by ignoring what the other is saying and completely shutting down.

In a Giver–Giver rhythm both of you are trying to "win." In fact, however, the two of you inevitably lose when you get caught in this deadly game.

Giver–No Receiver: The second non-rhythm occurs when there is a *Giver* with *No Receiver*. This often takes place between parents and children, or teachers and students. It also happens when the desired Receiver is preoccupied with another matter. You have experienced this situation frequently. For instance, you were in that important staff meeting, setting goals for next year. You offered a marvelous suggestion (in your humble estimation). But nobody responded to it. No one even commented on it. The group simply went onto what the leader was saying. You felt like you didn't exist. You became discouraged and found yourself remaining silent for the rest of the meeting.

When you want to Give, and there is no one there to receive, you feel alone, frustrated and deflated. You may keep on trying to give. If you have no luck, then you do the same as Sylvia and Stan above. You repeat yourself, and you get louder, hoping the other wakes up and hears your profound statements on life, or, at least, your message that the garbage has to go out to the curb. Communication breaks down because you can't connect to a person who will not receive you. Many relationships eventually end when this dynamic operates regularly. The Giver wears out trying and backs away – often so far away that he or she no longer cares if you receive or not.

Receiver–No Giver: The third non-rhythm of communication occurs when you have a *Receiver* with *No Giver*. You want to know what the other feels or thinks. You ask, but get no response or an elusive reply. Parents of teenagers know this experience well.

The quasi-dialogue goes like this:

Parent: "Where did you go?"

Teen: "Nowhere."

Parent: "What did you do?"

Teen: "Nothing."

Parent: "Who were you with?"

Teen: "No one."

The parent is positioned to *receive*; the teen chooses not to *give*. Communication breaks down. Whenever you relate to someone who doesn't share easily, you run into this problem. You want to receive, but the other doesn't give. This non-rhythm occurs in power relationships, where the one with information doesn't tell you what is going on. If he has more information, he also has more power. You are in the dark, not sure what will happen next. You become dependent on him, waiting for him to reveal his information or take action so you can respond. You can't be pro-active in such a circumstance. You must wait and then react when new data are presented.

Having a Receiver without a Giver also hurts intimate relationships. The very nature of such a relationship includes *mutual* sharing. You want to know her, get inside of her spirit, her thinking and her feelings. But she doesn't open that up to you. You can't reach deep intimacy without both of you opening up and sharing, especially when one of you wants to receive. If you wish to know your partner and that person doesn't give, you feel hurt and alone. You believe you want this relationship more than she does. You may attempt many strategies to get your partner to "open up." In the effort, you most likely come across as a nagging or demanding person, which pushes the other away. Eventually you give up and back away yourself. Intimacy is lost because you and your partner created a non-rhythm of communication.

Receiver–Receiver: The fourth non-rhythm, *Receiver–Receiver*, happens infrequently. If both of you are anxious to understand and listen to each other, then neither stands in a Giving position. Not much transpires. At times, this dynamic takes place in a classroom, when a teacher wants to know what students think on a topic, but the students don't feel they have enough information to respond. After the question is posed, silence reigns. The teacher wants to receive the students' knowledge, while the students sit there still wanting to learn from the teacher. Communication breaks down because both parties seek to learn and nobody wants to teach.

As I said, this non-rhythm doesn't happen much. We need not spend time with it here. I present it because it makes logical sense that such a non-rhythm could happen. But in the practical order, the other three non-rhythms cause the most difficulty. Once you get them going, they are difficult to stop. You need to consciously interfere with such non-rhythms and attempt to create the dynamic of a *Giver* and a *Receiver*.

By keeping in mind the various rhythms and non-rhythms of Giving and Receiving, you are able to identify when your communication is on track and when it's breaking down. Once you recognize which non-rhythm you have been involved in, you can then make adjustments to regain the only communicating rhythm that works – having a *Giver* and a *Receiver*.

Rhythm of Communication

Giver – Receiver

Non-Rhythms of Communication

Giver – Giver

Giver – No Receiver

No Giver – Receiver

Receiver – Receiver

Chapter Two

Principles and Tools for Communicating

Principle 1

Approach every communication as though the other
doesn't know about Giving and Receiving.
You, then, must assume responsibility for creating a
Giver-Receiver rhythm.

No matter how much the other knows about communication, how natural he is at it, how many workshops on it he has been to, it's best for you to assume responsibility for creating the Giver–Receiver rhythm. In the intensity of the communicating moment, it's up to you to recognize what is going on. If the other is poised to give, then you need to receive. If you sense the other's openness to receive, then you can give.

If you insist that the other receive your important message when he wants to be giving, you create a Giver–Giver non-rhythm. You cannot demand that the other change to fit your communication needs. You cannot insist that he listen to you if he is desperately trying to tell you something. First look to yourself to adapt and adjust. You have to change. Even if you want to tell him something. If you realize he is trying to get something across to you, then you must stop talking and listen first. Keep yourself focused on the Giver–Receiver rhythm. If you detect that he wants to give, then you receive. When he is capable of receiving, then you can give.

Imagine a wife and husband coming together for Christmas. Each has purchased a gift for the other. He comes to her holding boxes upon boxes of clothes. She comes to him carrying a large bag of golf clubs. They stand there, both in *giving* positions. Her arms are full of clubs, his full of clothes. He says, "Merry Christmas, Darling" and extends the boxes toward her. She replies, "No, no. Merry Christmas to you," offering the clubs to him. To push this a little further, he argues, "No, I said it first. So you take this." She comes back with, "But I bought this gift way back in September, so I should go first."

On it could go, each of them pushing their gifts upon the other, neither wanting to receive first. One of them needs the wisdom to see the problem and respond to it. He can't rely on or wait for his wife to "give in" and receive his gift. He has the responsibility to recognize the Giver–Giver non-rhythm and adjust.

So he puts down his armload of boxes. As he sets them aside temporarily, he becomes capable of receiving. His wife, Jenny, now becomes the Giver and Bob, the Receiver. She gives him the clubs, wishing him a Merry Christmas. He receives them, thanking her for the gift. A Giver and Receiver rhythm has been established. As soon as she gives Bob the clubs, her arms become free to receive. She changes from a Giver to a Receiver simply because Bob received Jenny first. Now he can set down her gift to him and pick up the boxes of clothes for her. As she becomes the Receiver, he can become the Giver.

Verbal communication fits this example almost perfectly. In it, you both think your message is more important to give first. So you take a giving stance. When you realize what is happening, you need to set aside *your* message temporarily. You put on hold your values, beliefs, feelings and opinions until you hear your partner's message. When she has completed her giving, then you can return to your own values, beliefs and feelings, and share your message with her.

You can hope that she will hear your point of view as you have attempted to hear hers. If, instead, she begins giving again while you're giving, then you become a Receiver one more time. If this continues indefinitely and you realize she is only interested in giving, then you can attempt to structure her receiving. After you believe you have gotten her full message, let her know you have it and then ask her if she would like to know what you think about the topic. She will almost always say "yes." Encouraging the "yes" from her tends to invite more openness on her part to receive your message.

After she says "yes, I want to know," then you can proceed to tell. Most likely she will still jump in with an opinion or two. At that point you can stop her, saying "Wait a second, you shared your view of this, and I think I understand it. You said you wanted to hear my point of view, so please let me share it with you." This kind of structuring usually helps the other become a Receiver.

The purpose of communication is to unite people. Like the rest of us, you possess a deep longing to belong, to feel one with others, to pass your days on this earth well connected to friends. You communicate to bring joy to yourself and fulfillment to others. Realize your responsibility in creating the Giving–Receiving rhythm essential for effective communication. You will make it happen if you don't rely on the other person as the expert in communication skills. The expert must be *you*.

First, let's look at you as the *Giver* in communication. Then we'll explore you as the *Receiver* in the rhythm that connects you to others.

The Giver

Principle 2

You need to be self-revealing by sharing your thoughts and your feelings.

When you talk, you reveal something about yourself. You let the other person into your inner world of thoughts and feelings. Communicating thoughts appears easier than expressing emotions. Emotions feel less under your control. They also seem closer to your real self. If you express feelings, you sense that more of yourself is being shown. You feel more vulnerable revealing emotions, with the exception of anger. Different from all other emotions, anger doesn't generally show vulnerability. Instead, it demonstrates strength. Relationally it often serves to push others away rather than create intimacy. Interestingly, then, it's the emotion many people express readily. It helps maintain distance between people.

In many relationship programs the expression of feelings is encouraged. Marriage Encounter offers a perfect illustration. The couple is asked to reflect on a question, for example, "What was your parents' marriage like?" Attached to the question and to every question asked in Marriage Encounter is the follow-up question, "And how does that make you feel?" The belief in these programs is that by sharing feelings, you increase intimacy. Generally this is true.

However, for a number of people (more commonly for men than women) the question "How does that make you feel?" may become an obstacle to communication. Not all people represent their inner or outer world through their feelings. Many use pictures or sounds to identify their experiences. Neuro-linguistic programming (a practical system that focuses on the process of interaction between people) has helped us understand that each person has a dominant way of taking in outside realities and representing those experiences inside the mind.

Basically there are three ways you bring the outside world into your mind and experience it:

1. You can create pictures in your mind of what is happening in the outside world. For example, you might *see* your kindergarten teacher and classroom when you think back that far.
2. Or you can hear sounds and voices as you reconstruct what is happening out there. You might *hear* your teacher's gentle voice as she welcomed you to school.
3. Or you can represent the outside world through you feelings. When you remember kindergarten, you might experience a scary *feeling* creeping into your stomach.

Because of these different ways of representing the outside world in your mind, the question "How does that make you feel?" may not fit for someone who represents through pictures or words.

Understanding this notion helps you realize the need to develop all three modes of representing and expressing yourself. If your dominant mode of expressing yourself is through feelings, but your friend takes in through pictures what you share, you may miss each other's messages to varying degrees. You help your communication skills by developing the ability to express yourself in pictures, sounds and feelings. You want to tell the other what you *see* in your mind's eye, what you *hear* within and what you *feel*.

Put simply, to communicate well you need to share your thoughts (in pictures and inner sounds) and your feelings. Because thoughts seem easier to share, you tend to use them more frequently. Trying to gain a balance between expressing thoughts and feelings is the best approach to take. If you only share thoughts, you place limits on how deep the relationship can go. You may tell someone you *think* she is very nice. You believe she has a great personality. You see her as a social, caring person. But such statements do not have the power of intimacy that a feeling statement has, such as "I love you."

In all your relationships, you decide how close you want to be to the other person. You self-reveal only to the degree of closeness you want to achieve. Certainly you won't share many of your inner thoughts and feelings with the television repair person. On the other hand, to create a personal, loving relationship with another, you will focus more on sharing your feelings than simply your thoughts and opinions about world affairs. You control the level of intimacy in relationships by the degree of talking you do. The more you reveal your inner life, the more intimate you become.

If self-revelation seems scary or difficult for you, then you need to practice it. Begin by paying attention to how you represent the world to yourself. Do you have pictures in your head? Do you hear voices in dialogue? Or do you have a feeling in response to an experience? Notice how you express yourself:

"I *see* what you mean."

"What do you *see* in him?"

"What is your *vision* of the project?"

"I *heard* the message in that story."

"I need to *talk* this through in my mind."

"I *sensed* what you were saying."

"I *feel* we'll win."

These expressions and others like them cue you to the way you represent and express yourself. Notice the same things about your friend or partner. Try communicating in the way you think he or she might best receive you. If your friend is a visual person, tell him your anger toward your boss is like a tornado busting up houses and throwing around cars as it races through you. He can see that in his mind. Of if you are talking with a feeling person about your daughter's basketball game, you might say, "The tension in the gym was sky-high. My stomach was churning away the entire time." She can identify with that feeling.

If you try sharing feelings, beware of the word "that." If you hear yourself saying, "I feel *that* you did better than he did," you have expressed a *thought*. "That" always indicates a thought is coming, even if you say "I feel . . ." before it. To express a feeling leave the word "that" out of the sentence. "I feel *sad* you lost." Now, you are expressing a feeling.

If you find yourself more frequently expressing thoughts than feelings to your friend, challenge yourself to verbalize your feelings. First, identify what you feel; then label it (put a name on it); and finally say it, "I feel sad, or excited, or calm or nervous." Keep the word "that" out of your expression of feeling. Remember, the more you share your thoughts and feelings with someone, the more intimate you become. You control the level of intimacy, because you control the words that express your inner life.

Principle 3

" Small talk" is important in any relationship.

At the beginning of most intimate relationships you make "big talk." You start by discussing your pasts, your goals, your futures. At some point, you reveal some of your limitations to see if the other will accept you as you are. When he does, the relationship accelerates. Such deep conversations make your heart beat faster and add excitement to your life. But they also exhaust you. You stay up until 4:00 o'clock in the morning, getting "into each other's space."

As you get to know each other, the seriousness of the relationship eases up, and you begin having fun together. You enjoy doing things with each other and become interested in the ordinary events occurring for one another. Over time, as your relationship deepens, intense conversations will continue but not as frequently as when you first came to know each other. There probably is simply not as much to talk about. You know so much about each other. Furthermore, you learn how to communicate with one another in many non-verbal and intuitive ways. Also, as the relationship grows, you "de-focus" it. It feels secure and in place. You can now turn your attention outward, zeroing in on your careers, children, other interests and friends.

I certainly am not suggesting you no longer need to pay attention to your relationship. You must always attend to that. But because you have shared deeply and seriously, you now trust the strength of the relationship. Instead of looking at yourselves, you pay attention to the scenery out there. When your relationship becomes troubled, you turn back in upon yourselves, as you did in the early days of getting to know each other.

In most relationships light chatter is a sign of health. You're interested in your wife's visit to her mother. You ask a friend how the golf game went. You inquire about your daughter's exam. And so on. Small talk includes conversation about everything: the neighbors, the local sports teams, office workers, the boss, the weather, a book you finished, the television show (certainly soap operas), the brakes on the car. The list goes on.

Over the years I have heard some people, mostly men, say they don't like small talk. It's a waste of time. It bores them. They don't care about the neighbor's kids or the bugs eating the beans in the garden. Generally I have noticed that these people don't engage in serious talk either. They simply do not talk. They use the small talk argument as an excuse not to talk at all.

If you fall into this category, please try to get used to small talk. Without it, no words will be spoken between friends. No relationship can be sustained by serious conversation alone. Small talk bonds you with another. It serves as a bridge between you. Without words the relationship drifts and eventually dies. When you don't use words to connect to your wife, she will tend to use even more words. Then you can easily complain, "She does enough talking for the both of us. I don't need to say anything." Not fair! Words, no matter how serious or how light, connect people. She keeps talking in order to stay connected. If you want her to tone down, then begin talking yourself. Light talk keeps you connected in a gentle, easy way.

To develop your "small talk" ability, try to remember the little things that happen during the day. Keep a notebook at the beginning just to remind you. Then tell your friend or partner about these interesting events. Also, try to get enthused about what your friend has to say. When he or she is talking, try to focus on what is being said rather than drifting into your own thoughts. Small talk may seem small in a relationship, but it plays a giant part in keeping the bond firm and strong.

Principle 4

Complimenting, praising and encouraging another brings life to a relationship.

You work hard and spend considerable time and energy to get complimented by others. Clothes are not only worn for warmth, comfort and decency; you also choose them to draw attention, to enhance yourself in the eyes of others and to have people say how nice you look. You get your hair cut, permed, sprayed and dyed, your finger nails done, your face made up and your shoes shined, all in order to be noticed. When no one comments on how stylish you look, you feel like people didn't notice, and you are momentarily disappointed.

If appearances don't make any difference to you, then something else will. Perhaps your work. You want someone, preferably the boss, to notice and compliment you on the job you just completed. Certainly you'd like the compliment in the form of a raise. If work doesn't get you praise, then maybe your athletic skills will. On the golf course, you make a great shot. The other three players all tell you how well you did. And if they don't, you compliment yourself, often times out loud: "Boy, that really felt good. Nice shot, Dale."

So it is, you look for praise and compliments in various ways. We all do. The world is filled with us praise-seekers. Among us, then, we need some people willing to be praise-givers. In choosing that role, you give people something they truly desire. By giving praise, you satisfy a hunger in everyone for recognition. Noticing offers a gift we all want, but only ask for indirectly. We *hope* you will notice. When you do so, when you compliment, praise and encourage us, we will be drawn to you. Why? Because you give us something we need, namely recognition. You tell us we exist.

You would think praising and complimenting would flow easily because it's such an up-beat activity. Your positive words always make the other feel better. Then why do you not speak or hear so many compliments and positive statements?

I have found at least three reasons:

1. You are the center of your own world. If you're preoccupied with your own thoughts or work, you don't notice others. Obviously, the more centered you are in your own life, the fewer compliments you will pass out. Think of a time when you were worried about a test, a job, or your child, and someone began telling you about the promotion she just got because of the successful project she just completed. It was hard to feel happy for that person as long as you were focused on your own problem. To compliment and praise, you need to center on the life and experience of the other. As you know, that's not always easy to do.

2. Like so many of us, you were probably raised with the old moral imperative regarding humility. You were never to get a "big head." The corollary to that was, "And you should not give a big head to anyone else." You grew up

believing, then, that to compliment and praise someone would make him or her proud and that was not good. Nonsense! Most people would do well to have "big heads." People need to think well of themselves and to know that others think well of them, too. It doesn't take much to tell them they look nice, or they are doing a great job of parenting their children. Your compliment is a vitamin pill for their health. And it doesn't cost anything except your enthusiasm.

3. Jealousy keeps you from complimenting others. If you're in a relationship where you cannot delight in the other's successes and accomplishments, then you don't have a friendship, and the relationship can't grow. In this kind of relationship, competitiveness occurs, which disrupts the mutuality needed to make close friendships work. If you think comparatively, you will have trouble giving compliments. You will falsely believe that praising the other somehow makes you less than that person. The beauty of real friendship lies in being happy and excited for your friend's success.

To increase your complimenting ability, start by paying attention. Notice what others are wearing, how they look, what they're doing. Consciously look for ways to praise others and recognize them. This will make you feel better, and they will respond more positively to you.

I recently attended a seminar on computers and was struck by the instructor's ability to make us feel smart. We were all fairly "computer illiterate" at the beginning of the day. We were afraid to ask questions because it would show just how ignorant we were. But when the first courageous person asked his question, the instructor commented, "Now, that's a very good question, Tom." And proceeded to answer it. Tom felt "smart." If he could ask one "good question," maybe he could ask another. Maybe if Tom asked a good question, the rest of us computer idiots could ask some good questions too. Gradually we did so. Throughout the course the instructor complimented us for our questions, for following the material, for making DOS do the things we commanded it to do. (I threw in that little computer term just to let you know I'm now only "computer semi-illiterate.") Through his compliments and praise we all engaged the computer more fully and came away from that program with the energy and confidence that we could master this machine.

Along with noticing others' activities, pay attention to your jealousies. If you tend to get jealous of others' successes, explore your beliefs. See how often you're comparing yourself with others. The more you do so, the more jealous you become and the less compliments you will offer. Challenge those beliefs. Try breaking free from comparative thinking by consciously realizing that others' successes don't change you at all. You were the same before their success as you are after. Your sense of worth doesn't depend on being better or worse than someone else. You are your own unique self, independent of other people's achievements or failures. You need to affirm your value without comparing yourself to your friend or neighbor. (More about this issue in the **Life Skills Series** book, *Accepting Yourself.*)

Principle 5

**In general, expressing thoughts and feelings
spontaneously and quickly adds
positive energy to relationships.**

Sometimes the most invigorating conversations are those where the mouth says immediately what the mind thinks. In fact, you may be one of those many people who think best *during* a conversation. I know I'm like that. I used to place a micro-cassette tape recorder in my pocket when I delivered a talk, because I often got new insights while talking out loud. The insight developed as the words came out of my mouth. In fact, I'm not sure if the words came before the thoughts or the other way around.

As you grew up, you probably lost aspects of your spontaneity. You learned how to "stop and think" before acting or saying what was on your mind. Often, of course, prudence dictated such control.

Unfortunately, the loss of spontaneity can lead to a boring, gray life of routine. It also causes distance in a relationship. You may hold back from expressing your love for the other; you may hesitate to let the other know your sadness over a loss in your own life; you may refrain from sharing your feelings as you watch the beauty of a sunset together.

Developing verbal spontaneity can bring a depth and intensity to the relationship that wasn't present before. In group therapy we often use a technique to help people become more verbally spontaneous. We ask each person what he or she is thinking, feeling or experiencing *right now*. We often have to encourage people at first, but gradually they become more and more skilled in saying what they are experiencing in the here and now.

Verbally expressing yourself spontaneously can, at times, present problems. When your immediate experience is anger or rage, then control and wisdom may lead you to slow down your response and moderate the manner in which you express your feelings. Generally any expression that creates more distance in the relationship should be controlled and modified in a way so that the other person can hear the message. You may have to stop and think how you can send it in a way that doesn't alienate the other and cause greater difficulties in the relationship.

Most other experiences can be shared spontaneously. These expressions draw you together because they reveal the real self in the here and now. Whenever you show your *real* self, it opens the door to intimacy.

To express yourself spontaneously, you need to be aware of what you're experiencing. So you have to stop yourself now and then, and ask yourself: "What am I experiencing *right now?*" You can do this anytime: when you're talking with someone; when you're alone driving from work at the end of the day; or when you're out walking the dog. Awareness is the key to spontaneity.

Try sitting with a close friend and have a "set-up spontaneous" discussion. Agree to try being aware of whatever thoughts pop into your mind and say them. Also attend to whatever feelings you might have and express those as well. Not only can this lead to deeper levels of relating, it can also be a lot of fun. For more information on exercises like this, see Chapter Three of this book, *Developing this Skill with Others*.

Principle 6

**Present messages in a way the other
can receive them.**

In the 1960s and 1970s the human potential movement encouraged honesty in communication between people. People were invited to "tell it like it is." Some gurus of the day even recommended "brutal honesty." Sensitivity groups thrived on these notions. Being honest and telling the other whatever was on your mind indicated a free spirit. This was considered healthy. As with most things, this honesty effort had pluses and minuses.

We were coming out of a psychologically repressive era. People kept their thoughts and feelings to themselves. Parents didn't believe in showing affection in front of their children, nor did they argue in their presence. If a wife felt hurt or ignored by her husband, she toughed it out as a "good wife" would. If a husband worried about the business, he kept it to himself so as not to worry his wife.

When you suppress your thoughts and feelings, you usually end up repressing them as well. In other words, when you cannot express your inner responses, you begin to lose touch with them. It's like having chronic back pain that's not too severe. If you can't do anything about it and you decide complaining doesn't help, you gradually learn to live with the pain. Living with it seems to reduce it. Basically, you accept it as part of your life and stop focusing on it so much. It doesn't go away, but you lose awareness of it much of the time.

By encouraging you to express yourself, to be honest, the human potential movement was calling you to get in touch with your thoughts and feelings. To express yourself honestly, you had to pay attention to what you were experiencing. Honest expression certainly appeared helpful and a good idea.

But what happened to the one receiving the honest, at times brutal, expression? If the "honesty" was filled with anger and venom, the receiver often had trouble hearing the message. The Receiver was devastated by the "sharing," while you, the Giver, felt great for having spoken your truth.

A number of years ago while I was directing a social service center, a verbally aggressive staff member announced to me he was going to have a talk with our secretary about her work for him. She came into my office and told me Fred wanted to talk with her and she felt scared. That afternoon they had their talk. When it was over, Fred returned to my office beaming, saying he felt very good about their conversation. "I got everything off my chest that I wanted to say. I think it was a wonderful session." Shortly after he left, the secretary came into my office in tears, wanting to quit because she could no longer take such "verbal abuse."

Did these two people communicate? Not very well. It was from this experience that I learned the importance of saying things in a way the other could receive them. I realized I had to think about what I wanted to give and what the other was capable of hearing. If I only concerned myself with being honest and saying whatever I thought, I could actually end up communicating *dishonestly,* even though my goal was to tell it like it was. How so?

If, for example, you communicate in too strong a manner, the other may block what you're really saying because it's too hurtful. She may then take your words, work them around in such a way so that she can handle them. In so doing, however, she distorts your message. Now truth has not been communicated. Is that her fault or yours? I think both. While you cannot be sensitive to every possible way of hurting another's feelings, you do need to pay attention to the manner in which you say things if you want the other to understand you. On the other hand, she, ideally, needs to see past her own sensitivities and recognize what you are really trying to say. Yet you cannot rely on her doing that. You have no control over her sensitivities. So you need to watch your own manner of communicating.

Janis wanted an honest talk with Robert. She told him, among other things, that this relationship would not have a future if he kept drinking. She wasn't going to tolerate it. She said he had no respect for her and was only concerned about himself. She also told him, in the midst of this, that she loved him and wanted the relationship to last. She said all this with considerable anger and volume. She had never talked to him this way. He was floored. So he blocked out most of what she had to say. He only heard the part about her not respecting him. Oops! That's not even what she said. She said *he* had no respect for her. Apparently, he couldn't hear that part and turned it to mean that she had no respect for him. He had distorted her honest communication. Now they were further from the truth than when they had started. They had, in fact, communicated dishonestly.

In this case Janis needed to pay closer attention to what Robert was able to receive. Perhaps she needed to assure him of her love right from the beginning of the conversation. She may have needed to talk more about herself and about her care for him than about what was wrong with him. She could have said, "You know I love you and want our relationship to be a long and happy one. I do, though, get very concerned about your drinking, and I worry that it might have a bad effect on our relationship." Period. One message at a time might be all Robert could handle. After he got that message, she might have been able to tell him how she felt when he didn't seem to respect her.

Is this walking around on egg shells? I don't think so. I think it means you're willing to *honestly and carefully* communicate with your friend, so that mutual understanding goes on. If you want to bang the other over the head, if you want to hurt him or her, then fine, you can speak with little regard for what the other is able to hear. But if you really want to make contact and get your point across, then you need to speak in a way the other can receive.

Finally, I hope you realize the delicate balance between this principle and the one above. There I discussed the helpfulness of speaking spontaneously. Here I am wanting you to be careful about what you say. Generally, you can speak spontaneously if the relationship is strong and both of you feel good about yourselves and each other. Also, spontaneous expression of positive, light thoughts and feelings is almost always well received. You need more sensitivity in speaking with another if he is not feeling good about himself or if the relationship is antagonistic.

To develop this aspect of communication, first assess the relationship. If you're confident of its underlying strength and feel you're both on the same side, then you need not worry too much about what you say and how you say it. If you judge the relationship to be weak or antagonistic, then reflect on what the other can hear before saying it.

Second, ask yourself how *you* would feel if the *other* said what you are about to say. If you would not want to hear it, then try saying it in other ways that might make it more palatable. Be careful, however, about using yourself as the norm for the other's reaction. Just because it might not bother you doesn't mean it won't bother the other.

Principle 7

**When you have a problem with another,
speak about it as *your* problem.**

If you have a difficulty with another person, whose problem is it? Yours or hers? It's yours. I know it often seems like the problem is the other's. But it really belongs to you. You need to own it. Try not to lay it on the other. Talk about it as your problem, not hers. If someone comes late to a meeting and you're upset, you have the problem. If your children play the stereo full blast and it drives you crazy, you have the problem. They love the stereo on high.

When addressing *your* problems with the other person, it works best to talk about them precisely as belonging to *you*. When you're annoyed with your co-worker's behavior, it's very easy to blame him and focus on how wrong he is. You will tend to tell him so in a way that he can't hear. You might say, "Darn it, Jack, anyway. *You* are so slow in getting those reports done. *You* have no discipline. *You* have no motivation. *You're* slowing down everybody's work. Get it together, and get going."

That approach is called sending "You messages." Instead, you need to send "I messages." You might say, "Jack, *I* have a difficult time getting my work done when you don't finish on time. *I* need you to complete your reports on time, so *I* can do my job. Help *me* out, Jack. Please get that report to me by Friday. Thanks."

In this approach Jack won't feel attacked and won't need to defend himself. You're approaching him with *your* difficulty and asking him to help you out. He is more apt to hear your message asking for help than if you tell him how inadequate he is. So be sure you own your own problems and present them to others as your own. You will get a much better hearing and a more positive response.

Principle 8

**Use non-sexist language to maintain a sense of
mutuality and equality in your relationships.**

This attitude applies primarily to men but has significant implications for women as well. When you learned English as a child, you were taught "he, his, him" to represent all people. It was "mankind" and "chairman" and God was "Our Father." You didn't mean to exclude women. You didn't consciously think less of women because of those little words. However, buried deep within our culture and history, using male terms for all people did, and does, in fact, mean something. It declares the dominance of men. It means the way our culture expresses itself is through male language and the male viewpoint.

In personal relationships that dominance has continued. Men have overtly dominated women. Stronger, more assertive and aggressive, men have generally had the upper hand. With such a one-up position, mutuality, and thus intimacy, have been more difficult to attain in heterosexual relationships.

Language reflects attitudes and beliefs. Today women are fighting for a sense of equality with men. One expression of that equality lies in the language men and women use. Trying to become more sensitive to the use of language has several effects. First of all, it says that the man respects and values the position of women in society as well as in relationships. Second, it shows respect for the efforts of women to be recognized as equals. Third, it creates a heightened sensitivity in the man's mind regarding women as people with rights.

Using the language another desires speaks volumes to that person about respecting, honoring and dignifying the individual. Even if you don't personally believe saying "mankind" makes any difference, if it matters to women, that alone would be sufficient reason to use non-sexist language. We all learned this lesson from the black community. For many white people, saying "black" instead of "colored" made little difference. However, to black people it signified a change in their self-perception and self-respect. "Colored" became a derogatory term. So the change was made to "black." If a people or a sex seeks such a language change because it reflects an attitude shift, then it helps to respect that change and honor that desire.

Over the years you have probably become comfortable with calling black people black. Now when someone calls a black person "colored," you flinch internally. It no longer fits. Internal flinches are positive signs that you're changing, becoming more sensitive to another's view and dignity. Your awareness of male dominated language needs also to cause a flinch when you hear it. Getting to this point helps you honor and regard women as equals. The majority of women want to be included in "humankind." Women, in fact, serve as "chairpersons" and "committee women." By adjusting your language, you first tell yourself that they are equal and one with men. Second, you announce to them that you recognize them as equals. In that kind of equality, you gain a richer sense of mutuality. Such sensitivity can only serve to enhance the closeness of your relationships.

To develop a sensitivity in this area, listen to other people's language, be it in personal conversations, on television or on the radio. Try to pick up on the male references that supposedly include women as well. Simply become more and more aware. Listen to your own language. Try catching yourself whenever you use sexist words. Through your efforts toward awareness, you will gradually experience that inner flinch.

When you catch yourself about to say "he, his, him," as it applies to women as well, try saying instead "his or hers, him or her, he or she." Also try to use "humankind, chairperson, firefighter, congress person" and so on. This may feel clumsy. But remember, your effort to use the language others desire helps them appreciate you more and helps you gain deeper sensitivity to them. That can only increase the likelihood of deeper relationships.

The Receiver

Principle 9

In listening *slow down* your internal processes and seek data.

The key to effective listening lies in your ability to *slow down* inside. Often you race around inside your mind looking for something vital to say, or you hear yourself disagreeing before the other person has fully stated his or her belief. Your quick response or interruption of someone are signs you're going too fast inside. Instead of knowing what she will say before she says it, can you lay back and take a deep breath? Can you let her take you through the many trails of her mind guiding you to the heart of her matter?

By slowing down internally, you increase your chances of gaining more *information*. By doing so, you lessen the probability of *interpreting* the other person's statements. Judgments and interpretations tend to close off your listening ability. Once you have formed judgments during the communicating process, you cease acting as the Receiver and become, instead, the Giver.

Often in dialogue you feel a strong urge to *give* information, opinion and advice. You may listen but only for the sake of talking. You become a good listener only by corralling your desire to give messages. In dialogue, you need to believe your chance to give will eventually come around.

Principle 10

The more information you have, the less interpretation you do; the less information you have, the more interpretation you do.

Understanding the relationship between information and interpretation is helpful. Whenever you make a choice to respond to a person or situation, you need a certain amount of data. If you don't have enough hard information, you supply what is missing by reaching for your own personal view and experience. When people talk to you, they usually do not offer you one hundred percent of the available information. They leave blank spaces in their sentences. Your tendency is to fill in those blanks from *your own* experience. Sometimes you guess right and sometimes not.

When you fill in the missing blanks in another's message, you add *interpretation* to *information*.

Data Needed for Responding

The less information you have, the more interpretation you add:

INFORMATION	INTERPRETATION

Increase information to reduce interpretation:

INFORMATION $\rightarrow \rightarrow \rightarrow \rightarrow$	INTERPRETATION

In this figure you can see the relationship between information and interpretation. Since you need the whole block of data to respond to a situation, you must fill in some of the blank spaces of information with your own interpretation. As you can see, the more information you have, the less interpreting you need to do.

Your interpretations arise from within you rather than from the outside world. To interpret, you mix some sensory data, some stereotypic beliefs, some emotions, some guesses, some self-concept and some values. If your interpretations fit what the other person leaves unsaid, you guess well and should bond to that individual. If the interpretations don't fit that person's reality, misunderstanding results.

You hear a business associate say, "I really don't like making those phone calls to clients." If you don't seek more information, you add your own interpretations about the meaning of his statement. You may fill in the missing blanks with, "Then, he will not make those calls." You respond to your interpretation and become angry with him for not doing his job.

If you stay out of your world of interpretations and slow them down, you will gather additional information from him. By staying with him in his world, you will understand how fearful he is about making those phone calls. Knowing he must make the calls tomorrow already causes anxiety today. He still intends on making the calls but doesn't like doing it.

Now your interpretation and response are considerably different. Instead of anger you respond with compassion and support. And you remain connected because he feels that you understand.

Trying to gain more information always serves you well in communicating with others. To do so, you need to deliberately slow down your thoughts and reactions so you can stay with the other. Although this takes considerable discipline, the bonding that occurs is well worth the effort.

When you begin communicating with someone, tell yourself to

"go slowly." Try to form the attitude of really wanting to know what the other thinks and feels, even if you believe you already know. Stay with the facts. Stick closely to what that person is saying, without trying to anticipate or guess what's behind the words. Simply track with the person's expression of self.

Observe your ability to slow down your mind when you watch the evening news on television. Generally you watch calmly, making few judgments and interpretations, only perceiving the information given. Then when something catches you emotionally, you begin judging and interpreting. Notice this dynamic so you can become aware of it when you're in dialogue with another. Then practice watching television news, disciplining yourself to perceive without judging even in those instances when your mind starts racing ahead.

Principle 11

**Realize that the first words out of another's mouth are
not necessarily accurate reflections of
his or her inner life. Be patient.**

None of us is so in touch with our inner life that every verbal expression matches perfectly with what we really think and feel. The words that come out of your mouth may be over- or understated. Especially when you feel strongly, your expressions may not always match your "true" beliefs. How often have you been in conversations where you regretted saying something, or wish you had the opportunity to say it in a different way?

When listening to another, then, it helps to once again slow down and be patient with the other's effort to communicate exactly what he or she really wants to share. When somebody begins talking with you, try to think of his or her mind as a maze. At the center of the maze lies the real message to be communicated. When John opens his mouth and speaks to you, you stand together at the "starting point" of his mind's maze.

Your job, as Receiver, is to let him take you through that maze, hitting dead ends and circling around the outer edges until he comes to the center. You can't assume that his first words express accurately and fully the message at the core of him. If you just stay with John, tracking through his mind, he has a better chance of reaching his center, and you have greater odds of understanding him. It may take him four or five tries to "get it right."

In communication you often latch onto a word or phrase the other says. After that you may not hear anything else. A husband and wife argue. In the heat of the moment the wife says, "We never have any fun in our relationship anymore." He hears that and blocks on any other message she sends. He is now convinced she thinks the relationship is a complete bore and burden. He feels hurt and shuts her off, thinking to himself, "If that's how she feels, then I'll just back out of her life. If I'm so boring to her, I'll just go my way and she can go her way." End of conversation, and probably end of any closeness in the relationship.

If the husband could slow down internally and realize that the first verbal expression is not always the accurate one, he would listen further. His wife tells him that she has always had fun with him, but lately it seems like they are getting more serious as the kids are growing up. She misses the fun times they used to have and hopes they can regain those times again. That message sounds quite different from the first sentence reaching her husband's ears.

"But," the husband says, "why didn't she say that in the first place?" Well, because she thinks on her feet. She clarifies her thoughts while she speaks. She isn't always that in touch with her deeper thoughts and feelings. The point of her talking is to help her clarify her own thinking. To do so she needs her husband to hear her patiently and help her sort out her maze of thoughts and feelings.

This wife may also have unintentionally misstated a message by making it dramatic. She uses her opening message like a slap in the face. She exaggerates it. By overstating she brings her husband to attention. It takes a big person to get past those exaggerated messages because they are often hurtful. Yet her husband could offer a great gift by pausing, slowing down and saying to himself, "Wait. I just want to track through her mind until I'm sure her words match what she really wants to say."

You can work at collecting data and reducing interpretations by observing other conversations. Notice how frequently people re-say their same basic message. They are trying to put it in a way that matches their inner core. Notice the same in your own conversations.

When you listen to another, realize it may take a few attempts for the person to get the full message out. Generally when someone talks out loud, she clarifies her own thinking. So view conversation not as a finished thought process, but as a process of clarifying and getting in touch. That will help your patience.

Principle 12

**When listening, remain free from your own
views and beliefs temporarily.**

Developing this attitude and behavior might be the most difficult of all aspects of listening. Naturally you believe that your view of the world is based on reality. If you didn't believe your view to be true, you wouldn't hold onto it. Furthermore, you don't like other people misunderstanding you. When they do, you attempt to become the Giver, trying to straighten them out, and you stop receiving their messages.

To listen well, you need to set aside your beliefs, feelings, values, experiences and thoughts *temporarily*. By not focusing on your own position for the moment, you can more easily enter into the other's view. As you listen to another, you will hear a variety of self-talk taking place inside your mind: "That's not true." "He's always bragging about his son." "She spends so much money. She shouldn't have bought that." "Easy for him to complain about the kids. He's never here to take care of them anyway." When your beliefs and views remain active as you listen to another, they serve as filters letting in only parts of the other's message. And they color other parts of the message so you don't hear accurately. Also, by holding onto your own beliefs while the other shares, you are much more likely to cut in with your own view. Interrupting makes the other feel you have not truly heard his or her message. Communication breaks down.

I learned this principle well a number of years ago. While visiting my sister and her family on the east coast, we spent a day in Washington, D.C. Coming out of one of the museums on a hot August day, my ten-year-old niece, Sarah, said to her dad, "Daddy, I have a headache." Walking alongside her, I said, "Oh Sarah, I have a headache too." She turned to me and responded, "I don't care. I said it first." Although I heard her message, I stayed in *my* world with *my* headache. She wanted someone to step across into her world and be with her and her headache. Knowing I had a headache didn't help her with hers.

Remember your parents telling you what it was like when they were your age. Perhaps you do the same with your children. "Why, when I was your age, we used to walk to school two miles each way. And in the winter we didn't even have any boots, we were so poor." You say things like this when your children ask you to drive them to school, four blocks away, on a pleasant day. At that point they could care less about what it was like in the "old days." It's at times like these that you need to set aside your experiences and simply attend to the other's.

You need do this only *temporarily*. You don't want to throw out your view or compromise your values. Not at all. You only suspend focusing on and expressing your view until you have fully received and understood the other's view. Then you can return to your thoughts and share them with the other. In the example with my niece, I should first have set aside my own headache and listened to her complaint about hers. I could have said, "Oh, that's too bad." or "Gee, that must hurt." She then may have made another comment about how it felt. Then once I sensed she was finished being the Giver, I could have mentioned to her that I know how that must feel because I had a headache, too.

Setting aside your own agenda while listening to another becomes a special challenge at certain times:

1. *When you feel misunderstood.* At these times you tend to try correcting the misperception. You get stuck on the other's inaccuracy and want to jump in and fix his or her view.

2. *When your emotions are high.* Increased emotion almost always indicates a desire to be the Giver. One use of emotions is to present yourself to another with force or power. You use emotion to strongly state your position. Certainly you can see how this works with the emotion of anger. This emotion serves to inflate you before the other so she pays attention and hears you. Other emotions also seek expression. They urge you to give a message rather than receive one. This creates inner tension when you want to give but are trying to receive at the same time.

3. *When you are heavily invested in a relationship.* I can give parents wonderful advice about how to respond calmly to their children, but when it comes to my own children, it's much more difficult for me to follow my own rules. Because of my emotional involvement in their lives, I think I know what's best for them and how to best protect them from all evil and from making serious mistakes. So I don't listen to them as well as I might. I jump in with *my* position while they are trying to tell me theirs.

4. *When you feel threatened in some way.* If someone makes rejecting comments to you, criticizes you or verbally attacks you in any way, you tend to stop listening and want to speak back. You want to defend yourself by justifying your position or by attacking and invalidating the other person's remarks.

In these situations it becomes very important to temporarily set aside your own position and hear the other person to the end. Having allowed that individual to speak his mind, let him know you have heard. After that you can become the Giver and hope he will receive your message as you have received his.

It helps to practice this skill in non-emotional situations. Try setting aside the desire to give *your* advice, to tell *your* stories and to share *your* opinions when you're in the Receiving position. Have the attitude of honoring the other's world by attending to it fully, without bringing in your own incredibly wonderful experiences and wisdom.

Continue listening without referring to your own point of view until you feel the other has exhausted his or her message. At that point feel free to return to your message and give it to the other. You then have created the rhythm of Giving and Receiving.

After you have listened well in an emotional exchange, you may need to structure the other to hear you. Structuring goes like this: Some Givers just don't quit. You feel you heard the message, but they keep right on talking. At that point you can interrupt and say, "I really do understand what you are saying to me. (You can repeat the main theme again if you wish.) Now, would you like to know what I think about that?" By inviting the other to say "Yes", you orient him toward listening. He usually says, "Yes, tell me." Then you begin to share. He may jump right in on your message. If so, then you say, "Wait a second. I tried hard to hear you, and you said you wanted to know what I was thinking. So please let me finish." Asking the person if he wants to know and getting him to say "Yes" gives you leverage to remind him when he interrupts that he's the Receiver now, and you're the Giver. This is called structuring the other as Receiver.

Principle 13

**Realize that mental labels dictate the manner
in which you listen to others.**

The labels you hold in your mind regarding yourself and the person speaking determine how effectively you listen. You can attend workshop upon workshop on communication skills and still not communicate effectively. Why not? Because despite all the techniques you learn, the manner in which you view the other controls the way you respond. You throw your communication skills out the window when you form negative mental labels of yourself and/or the other.

In the past I have given many communication workshops teaching people "active listening." I have shown them how to respond to others, how to attend to body language and how to "reflect back" to the speaker what he or she was saying. What I missed in all these workshops was what happened *inside* these Receivers. All the while I was showing them communication techniques, they were carrying around images of the speaker and of themselves that influenced the way they communicated. If they saw the Giver in a positive light and saw themselves as *wanting* the information of the Giver, they automatically listened very well, whether they had "active listening" skills or not. They seemed to do it naturally.

On the other hand, when they labeled the speaker negatively, their listening skills dropped off considerably. They didn't want to listen to someone they distrusted, didn't like or perceived as ignorant. Furthermore, if they held negative views of themselves, they spent too much time worrying about how they were doing, while trying to converse with others. In their preoccupation to do well, they failed to listen with empathy.

Imagine going to a lecture by a person renowned in a field of interest to you. You get there, anxious to hear this wonderful and wise speaker. The label you apply to the speaker is "expert, brilliant, insightful and stimulating." The label you give yourself is "student, anxious to learn." The master of ceremonies quiets the crowd and announces that the speaker missed a plane and cannot make it in time. However, someone from the audience has volunteered to address the group on the same topic. He is introduced as a peer, with apparently no more knowledge than you have on the subject. Suddenly, you switch your labels. You see him as "Not knowledgeable, foolish for trying to match the master and unstudied." Your self-labels change as well. You perceive yourself as, "Knowing as much as he does, wasting your time here and angry the other speaker did not show up."

In the first scenario with the brilliant speaker, all of your labels facilitated an easy listening process for you. You are open and receptive, sitting on the edge of your seat, longing to take in the wisdom of the master. In the second scene all your labels change. While the speaker addresses the crowd, you engage in a lot of self-talk, challenging and criticizing the speaker. You don't listen well. The starting point for effective listening, then, lies in the view you take of yourself and the other.

You can *change* your labels, although not always easily. The best communication takes place when your labels are positive and respectful. When listening, try to create labels that include seeing yourself as a *student, open, desiring to know, seeking information, humble before the speaker, empty, ready to be filled* and so on. The most helpful labels for you to apply to the Giver or the speaker would include *expert, knowledgeable, master, valid, honest, caring* and so on. As a bare minimum, try to create an image of the other person as "attempting to speak what he or she believes to be true." Most people, most of the time, believe what they are saying, even if it contradicts your view of a situation. By giving them that much credit, you automatically become a better listener.

To dramatically improve your communication skills, spend a week paying attention to the labels you apply to others and to yourself when communicating. After a conversation, jot down the labels you discover of the other and yourself. Realize how positive and/or negative those labels are. Then see if the labels didn't determine the quality of your listening.

In those relationships where your labels of the other sound negative, write down positive labels that at least allow you to hear that person. Find positive labels that you can actually believe. Don't use a label that clearly contradicts reality. For instance, your friend always talks about herself. You realize you have labeled her as "self-centered." It would be hard for you to re-label her as "other-centered." But you could try viewing her as "insecure, and needing someone to affirm her." By shifting the label, you change your attitude toward the person, free yourself to listen and thus communicate with her in a more satisfying way.

Principle 14

Understanding is different from agreeing with someone and must precede agreeing. First attempt to understand, then proceed to agree or disagree.

If you didn't have a "judging faculty" within you, listening would be a snap. When you decide the speaker is "wrong" (your judgment), you stop listening. If you could give yourself a temporary lobotomy and interfere with that judging power, you would offer the speaker the wonderful experience of being heard and recognized. That's all most speakers want.

The need to separate judging from understanding becomes particularly important when the other person shares a problem with you. Most of the time that person wants you to first appreciate her difficulty. She wants you to feel some of her frustration or pain. Later on she may ask you what *you* think (time to agree or disagree). And much later she might ask your advice in helping her solve her problem. Do you notice the progression here? First, she wants you to *understand*. Second, she might want your *judgment*, agreeing or not. And third, she may seek your *problem-solving help*. That order is vital.

Because you're a caring person, the temptation is to immediately jump in to help the other out of her pain or difficulty. As soon as she begins sharing her problem, you're offering advice and solutions to the problem. This jumping ahead stands as the single biggest problem in communicating with a troubled person. In marriages, partners complain regularly about this dynamic. "He never just understands me," she laments. "He's always trying to tell me what to do or not to worry." She usually concludes this complaint with, "I don't want him to solve my problems or tell me I get too upset about these things. I want him only to tell me he sees how much this bothers me, and he can appreciate my difficulty."

Especially important in separating your judging and problem-solving from your understanding is your ability to allow the other person to have her own emotions. Again, because you care, you hate to see your partner feeling sad, anxious, upset, angry or hurt. When you see her caught in these emotions, you naturally try to lift her out of them. Please don't do that too fast. She is not asking you to free her from her feelings. She wants you to understand and dwell with her in her feelings. Saying things like, "You have no reason to worry," "Don't be sad," "It's no big deal," "You'll feel better in the morning," and "When you're like that, you should just go to bed," rarely help. In fact, the person feels less understood, and consequently her pain is increased because you aren't standing with her. She wants you to understand her; instead, you're telling her it's no big deal.

So, don't jump in to save the person who tells you a problem. Just listen and understand. The best way to respond to such a person is to follow the five-step process below:

Steps in Receiving

1. Hear the words being spoken.
2. Understand cognitively his or her point of view.
3. Appreciate that point of view. Get the *feel* of it.
4. Agree or disagree with it.
5. Try to solve the problem presented if that's an issue.

Sometimes you may hesitate to "just understand." By doing so, you wonder if you're giving the impression of agreeing with the other when you really disagree. Parents, in particular, often jump to disagreeing before understanding because their teenagers seem to equate the two processes. If the parents don't agree with their son's wishes to stay out till midnight, then the son accuses the parents of not understanding. It's an old teenage trick we all used on our parents. If you don't agree, you mustn't understand.

If you sense that the Giver thinks you're agreeing with him because you're empathically listening, then you can eventually correct that misperception. After you have spent some time just understanding, you can say, "Tom, I can really understand how you came to the conclusion to rob a bank rather than get a job, *but* I disagree with that conclusion." The word "but" moves you from the understanding step to the agreeing/disagreeing step.

Be careful not to disagree too early in the process though. If you wait patiently, you will get your chance to tell the other you can't agree with his point of view or his decision. When it comes to the other's emotions, however, there can be no agreeing or disagreeing. Emotions are simply there. You need to accept and understand the other's feelings without judging them. By disciplining yourself to always start a listening process with understanding, you help the other more fully than if you jump in too quickly with your problem-solving skills. Understanding is always more helpful than your advice.

That may be hard for you to appreciate if you're used to saving people from discomfort and pain. You want to get in there and fix something that isn't right. But with another's emotions, the best fixing takes place through understanding. Telling someone who's worried not to worry lets that person know you don't understand her. When she is carrying uncomfortable emotions, she feels alone and isolated. By understanding her, she feels connected to you. That feeling helps free her from her worry because she is no longer alone. I hope you get the sense of this because it's one of the biggest obstacles to good communication.

Principle 15

Effective listening, as well as sharing, is based on your *inner desire* to learn about and to stand with the other's unique experience of the world.

This attitude serves as a fitting conclusion to your understanding of communication. After all the principles and tools for communicating have been learned and practiced, the key to making it all happen lies in this attitude. No matter what skills or tricks you learn to communicate better, it's your inner spirit that makes the difference. If you really *want* to listen to and understand someone, then you will do so. Everything about you will be oriented toward that person. And the other will sense your presence and interest.

On the other hand, as the Giver you will share your deepest feelings if you truly *want* to. Your inner spirit will allow you to stand poised to give, to enter deeply into yourself and reveal what is there. If you desire to give what is in you, then you will do so. Ultimately giving and receiving are determined by your soul rather than by techniques.

Years ago, I attended a workshop on communication given by Charles Curran, a psychologist from Chicago, an expert in interpersonal relationships. He explained the meaning of communication by showing us the etymology of the word itself. "Comm," he explained, comes from a Latin prefix "cum." In English it means "with." "Unic" comes from an Anglo-Saxon word that means "Unique." And "ation" derives from a Latin suffix that in English connotes "action." Most words in English ending in "a-t-i-o-n" signal action of some sort. Generation, construction, destruction, adoration and so on are action words. I have since learned there is an exception to this rule. One word ending in "ation" does not connote action. The word? Constipation. (Just a little humor here.)

comm   –   unic   –   ation

with   unique   action

Communication, then, is a very *active* process whereby one person *stands with* the *unique* experience of another person. As you can see, this sounds more like listening than talking, more like Receiving than Giving. In attending to another, your spirit becomes one of standing with the unique thoughts, feelings and experience of the other person. After you have stood with the other, you can then invite the other to stand with you in your unique experience of the world as well.

So it is that your inner spirit moves you like the rudder of a ship, guiding you through the often treacherous waters of verbal communication. As long as you *want* to stand with another and *want* the other to stand with you, you will capture the essence of communication.

Approach any encounter, then, in the spirit of standing with the other person's experience. Get up close to the other's thoughts and feelings, trying to capture his or her inner perceptions of life.

If you have the chance, visualize the other person before speaking with him. Try to see him as a person of value, with an inner life that he experiences as unique and special to him. Try valuing his point of view, even if it differs from your own.

When you want to speak, let yourself feel the desire to be self-revealing. Know that verbal expression flows from inner conviction and awareness. By sharing your awareness of self, you join more fully with the other. Such union is clearly the most positive result of effective verbal communication.

Conclusion

Communication links people. It always involves a *Giver* and *Receiver*. Maintaining that rhythm is *your* responsibility. When the other *gives*, you must *receive*. When he or she is in a position to receive, you can give.

In developing your communication skills, start where the need seems greatest. You may decide your listening skills need the most work. Begin with *slowing down* your internal processes. Then work on letting go of your beliefs, views, values and feelings temporarily so you can stand with the other's experience.

If *giving* or sharing your thoughts and feelings seems difficult, begin by thinking of things to share and make small talk. Gradually, try getting to the revelation of feelings.

Commit yourself to getting better at this skill. Take one aspect of communication and work at it. Keep charts of how you are doing. Seek feedback from others. Reflect and assess daily on how you did, where you failed and succeeded. Learn from your mistakes. Remain optimistic. You can develop your communicating ability through hard work and discipline.

Is it worth it? Ask anyone who has talked with and listened to another human being, whether a business associate, customer, neighbor, relative, friend, child, lover, husband or wife. Ask anyone who knows the intimacy of deep friendship, who has experienced freedom from loneliness, who has known the security and delight of walking the earth's trails with a partner. Is it worth it? The answer is a chorus of "Yes," sung, chanted and shouted by all who have *Given* and *Received*.

Chapter Three

Developing this Skill with Others

While you can learn the theory of communication by yourself, you need other people to practice the skill of communicating. Working in a structured way with a friend or a group will improve your ability to communicate greatly. Here are some steps for working with others in order to improve your skill of communication:

Step One

Designate who will Give and who will Receive. You can only have one Giver at a time, but you can have several Receivers. Each of you take a minute and think yourself into your assigned role. Feel the spirit of giving or receiving.

Step Two

Begin sharing at cognitive levels and move to more feeling levels. Each of you take 30 seconds to one minute and share two *facts* about your life. The others receive the message.

Step Three

Advance from sharing facts about yourself to sharing:
- An opinion you have about anything.
- A story about your past.
- A political position you hold.
- A conviction you have.
- Something that made you sad.
- Something that made you happy.

Step Four

So far you have spoken and listened to each other without any *mutual* give and take. Now discuss one of the topics from the list above, but this time try to create the rhythm of mutual Giving and Receiving. After you have listened well to a person, then you can switch the roles and become the Giver, while the other receives you. Do this for a few minutes, then stop the process and evaluate how you did. Check to see if you got into any non-rhythms of communication, such as Giver–Giver, Giver–No Receiver, Receiver–No Giver. Did you feel understood by one another? Did you get to say what you really wanted to say?

Step Five

As you get more comfortable with the rhythm of Giving and Receiving, take a controversial subject, such as abortion, women's rights and roles, politics, religion or relatives, and discuss these topics. Try to establish a Giving–Receiving rhythm. Make sure you're slowing yourself down when listening and putting aside your own beliefs while attending to the other's.

Step Six

Discuss possible communication situations you will be having during the coming week with your spouse, children, co-workers or friends. If you have any potentially difficult circumstances approaching, you can role play them in the group. This is a wonderful way to practice your skills.

Step Seven

When you get together the next week or month, discuss your communication successes and failures since last you met. To do this effectively, it's helpful to keep some kind of written record of situations so you don't forget.

Step Eight

You can always use this book as the basis of a group discussion. Just take a principle and discuss what it means for you and how it can be applied in your life.

You will improve your communication skills rapidly when you work at it with others. You can help each other become aware of the rhythm of communication, of the attitudes and principles needed to make it effective. Your awareness will help you change the way you listen and the way you share. As you grow in your ability to communicate, you will feel more and more one with others and with the world around you. Such union will crown your life with a sense of fullness and contentment.

Appendix

Review of Principles
for Communicating

1. Approach every communication as though the other doesn't know about Giving and Receiving. You, then, must assume responsibility for creating a Giver–Receiver rhythm.
2. You need to be self-revealing by sharing your thoughts and your feelings.
3. "Small talk" is important in any relationship.
4. Complimenting, praising and encouraging another brings life to a relationship.
5. In general, expressing thoughts and feelings spontaneously and quickly adds positive energy to relationships.
6. Present messages in a way the other can receive them.
7. When you have a problem with another, speak about it as *your* problem.
8. Use non-sexist language to maintain a sense of mutuality and equality in your relationships.
9. In listening *slow down* your internal processes and seek data.

10. The more information you have, the less interpretation you do; the less information you have, the more interpretation you do.

11. Realize that the first words out of another's mouth are not necessarily accurate reflections of his or her inner life. Be patient.

12. When listening, remain free from your own views and beliefs temporarily.

13. Realize that mental labels dictate the manner in which you listen to others.

14. Understanding is different from agreeing with someone and must precede agreeing. First attempt to understand, then proceed to agree or disagree.

15. Effective listening, as well as sharing, is based on your *inner desire* to learn about and to stand with the other's unique experience of the world.